Super Cold

by Cas Lester
Illustrated by Bill Ledger

OXFORD
UNIVERSITY PRESS

In this story ...

Cam
(Switch)

Cam has the power to turn into different animals. Once she stopped some baddies from robbing a bank by turning into a giraffe.

Axel
(Invisiboy)

Slink
(Combat Cat)

Mee-OW!

Cam and Axel were in the sports hall. They were watching Slink show off some of his ninja moves.

"You're so cool, Combat Cat!" said Cam with a grin.

All of a sudden, they heard a distant crash.

"What was that?" cried Cam. They hurried out of the hall.

There was another loud crash.

"It's coming from Corridor B12, where the gadget storeroom is," Axel said.

"We're not allowed to go there," Cam replied. The gadget storeroom was full of things the Head had taken away from villains.

"But we have to find out what's happening!" Axel cried, rushing down the corridor.

Cam gasped as she looked down the forbidden corridor. "Someone has broken into the gadget storeroom!"

The storeroom's heavy, metal door hung open.

Cam spun into her superhero costume and became Switch. Axel became Invisiboy.

Just then, a peculiar-looking man stepped out of the storeroom. His skin was pale blue, and his head was covered in icy spikes of hair.

"Super Coldo!" exclaimed Switch.

Super Coldo

NUMBER 3 — MOST WANTED VILLAIN

Catchphrase: Freeze!

Hobby: ice sculpting.

Likes: iced buns, ice cream, I spy (say them out loud to see why!).

Dislikes: hot weather and radiators.

Beware! Super Coldo is a master gadget-maker. He once tried to freeze the whole city with his ice blaster. The heroes confiscated it and he went to prison.

"Stop!" shouted Invisiboy.

"No way!" Super Coldo was holding a long metal tube. "I've come to get my ice blaster back," he yelled.

"You should be in prison," said Switch.

"I escaped," replied Super Coldo.

"How?" asked Invisiboy.

"The same way I got in here," said Super Coldo, holding up a glistening piece of ice. "I used my ice key."

Suddenly, Super Coldo raised his ice blaster and fired it straight at the heroes.

"Look out!" shouted Switch.

Combat Cat dived in front of the children. A blast of ice hit him and froze him solid.

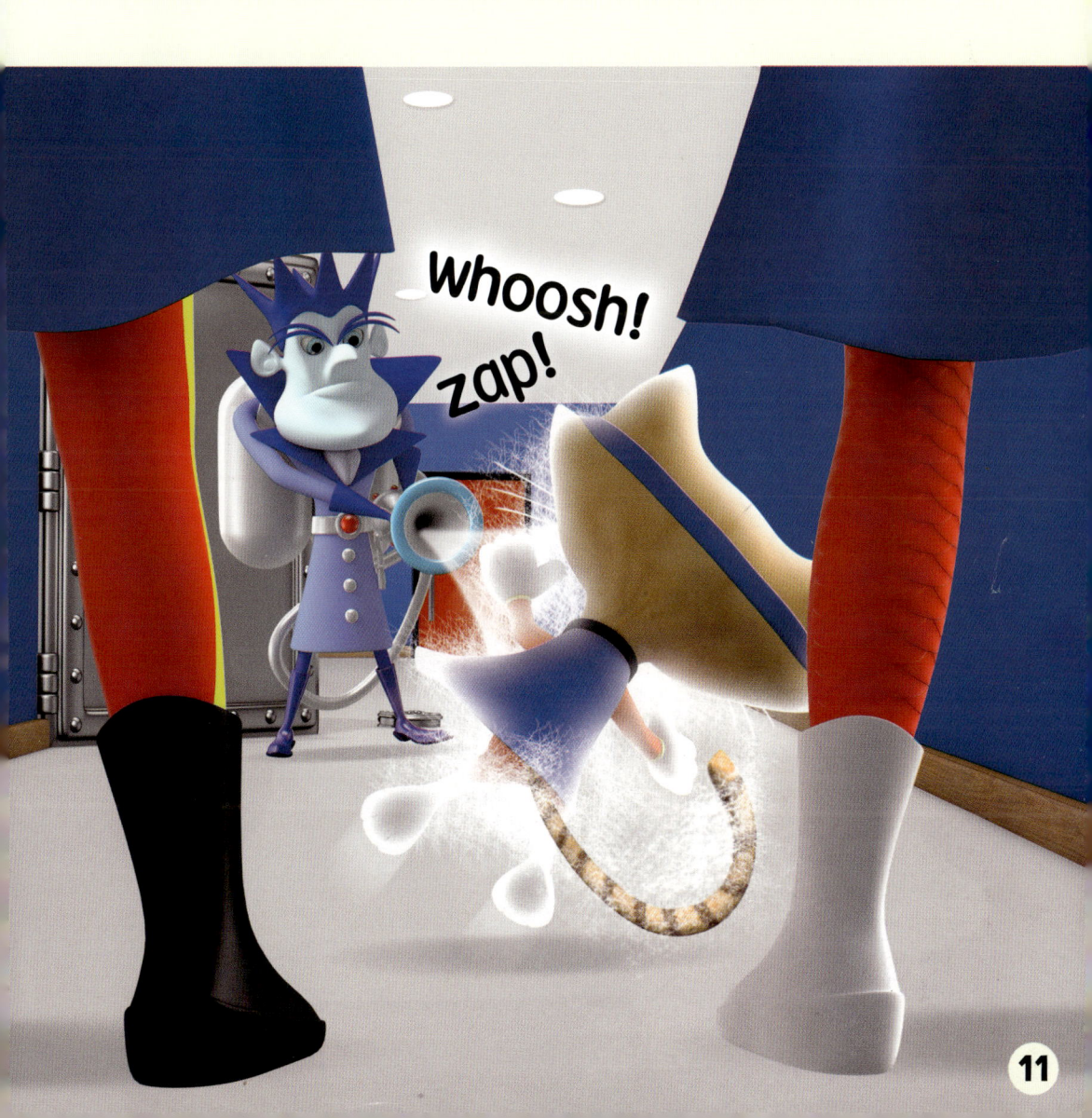

"You took something of mine. Now I am going to take something of yours," said Super Coldo. He undid Combat Cat's collar and put it in his pocket. Then he ran off. "Have an ice day," he joked.

Without the collar, the Head couldn't communicate with Combat Cat.

"Don't worry, Combat Cat," said Switch. "We'll get your collar back."

Switch and Invisiboy dashed past and began to follow the icy villain.

Hang on, what about me?

13

Super Coldo fired the ice blaster. The spray hit the floor and made a perfectly smooth sheet of ice.

Switch and Invisiboy slipped and skidded down the corridor.

Aaargh!

14

"He's getting away!" yelled Invisiboy.

"I have an idea," cried Switch. She changed into a dog. Switch quickly picked up the villain's scent and set off after Super Coldo. Invisiboy followed close behind.

Eventually, the scent led them to Super Coldo's hideout on the outskirts of Lexis City. It was a sleek, shiny building that looked like an ice cube.

Invisiboy noticed an open window. "Look," he whispered to Switch.

Switch had another idea. She turned from a dog into a cat ... that looked just like Combat Cat. Then she jumped through the window.

Invisiboy turned invisible and climbed in after her. Silently, they crept up on Super Coldo.

The silly villain was practising his sinister laugh in a mirror.

"Mwa-ha-ha-ha! Combat Cat and those heroes were no match for me!" he boasted. Super Coldo held up Slink's collar smugly.

Switch had heard enough. She leaped forward and tried to grab the collar.

Mee-OW!

"Combat Cat?" Super Coldo said, dodging out of the way. "But I froze you!"

Switch prepared to jump again.

Super Coldo grabbed his ice blaster. "I'll get you this time."

Switch was too quick. She darted between his legs. The villain tripped over and dropped the collar.

Invisiboy snatched up the collar.

Super Coldo saw the collar moving, so he knew Invisiboy was there.

"I'll get you, Invisiboy!" Super Coldo yelled, firing his ice blaster.

21

Invisiboy ducked. The ice ray missed him and hit the mirror instead. Then it bounced back and hit Super Coldo. He was frozen solid.

"You're going back to prison," Switch told Super Coldo.

"That'll cool him off," said Invisiboy, becoming visible again. Super Coldo couldn't move or speak, but he glared at them angrily.

23

By the time Cam and Axel got back to the academy, Combat Cat had started to thaw. Cam put Combat Cat's collar back round his neck. When the ice had melted a little, he smashed his way out with a kick.

"You really are a very cool cat," laughed Cam.